THE GREAT ARTISTS
Monet

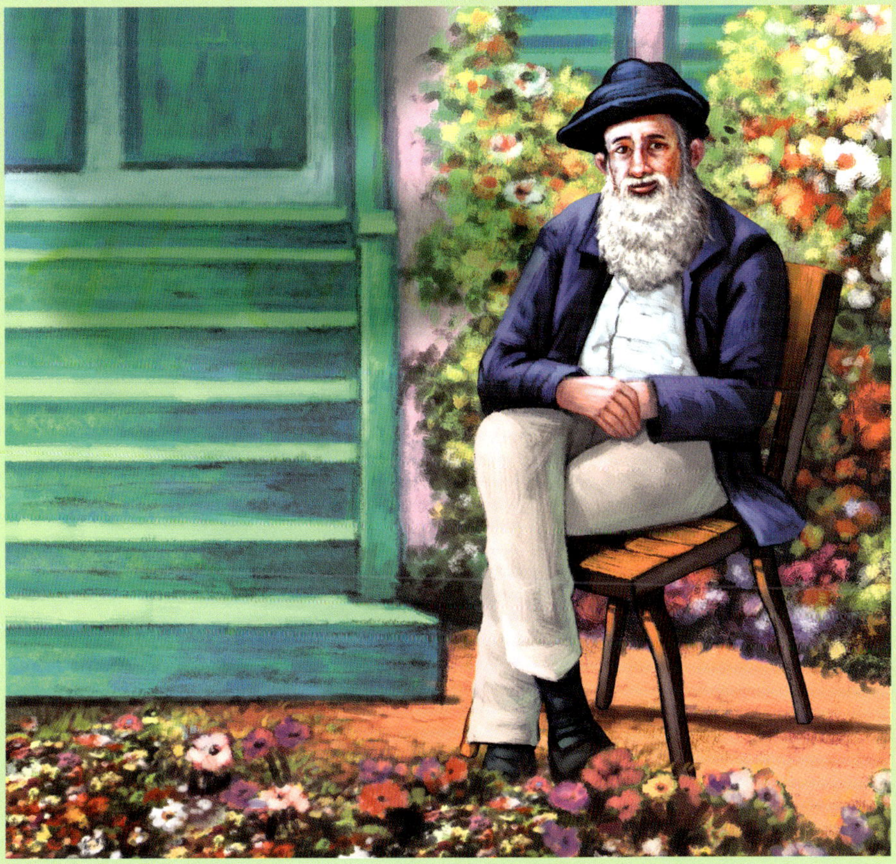

Om KIDZ
An imprint of Om Books International

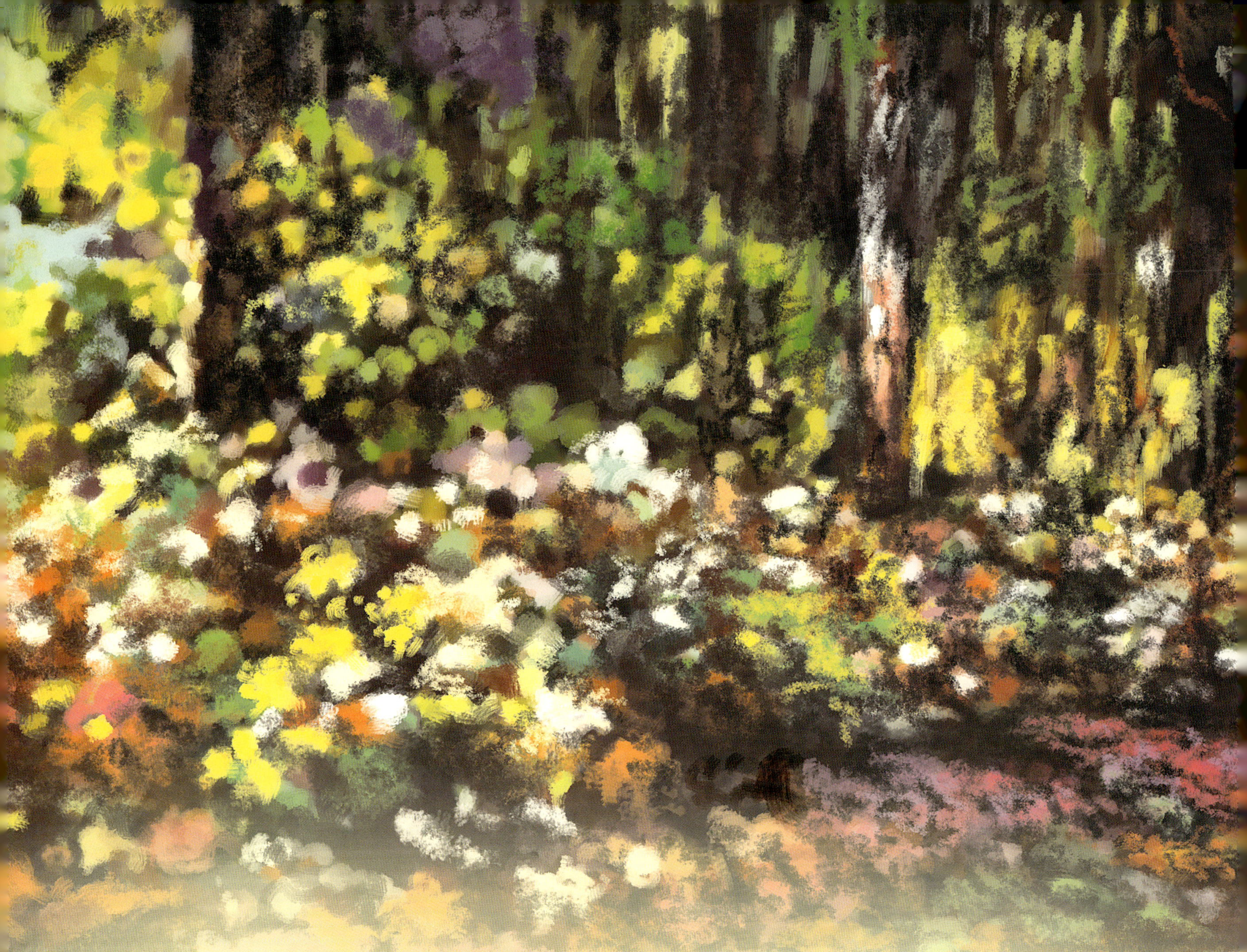

Oscar-Claude Monet was born on 14 November, 1840, in Paris, France. When Monet was 5 years old, his family moved to the seaside city of Le Havre. His father, Adolphe, worked in a grocery store and his mother, Louise, was a singer.

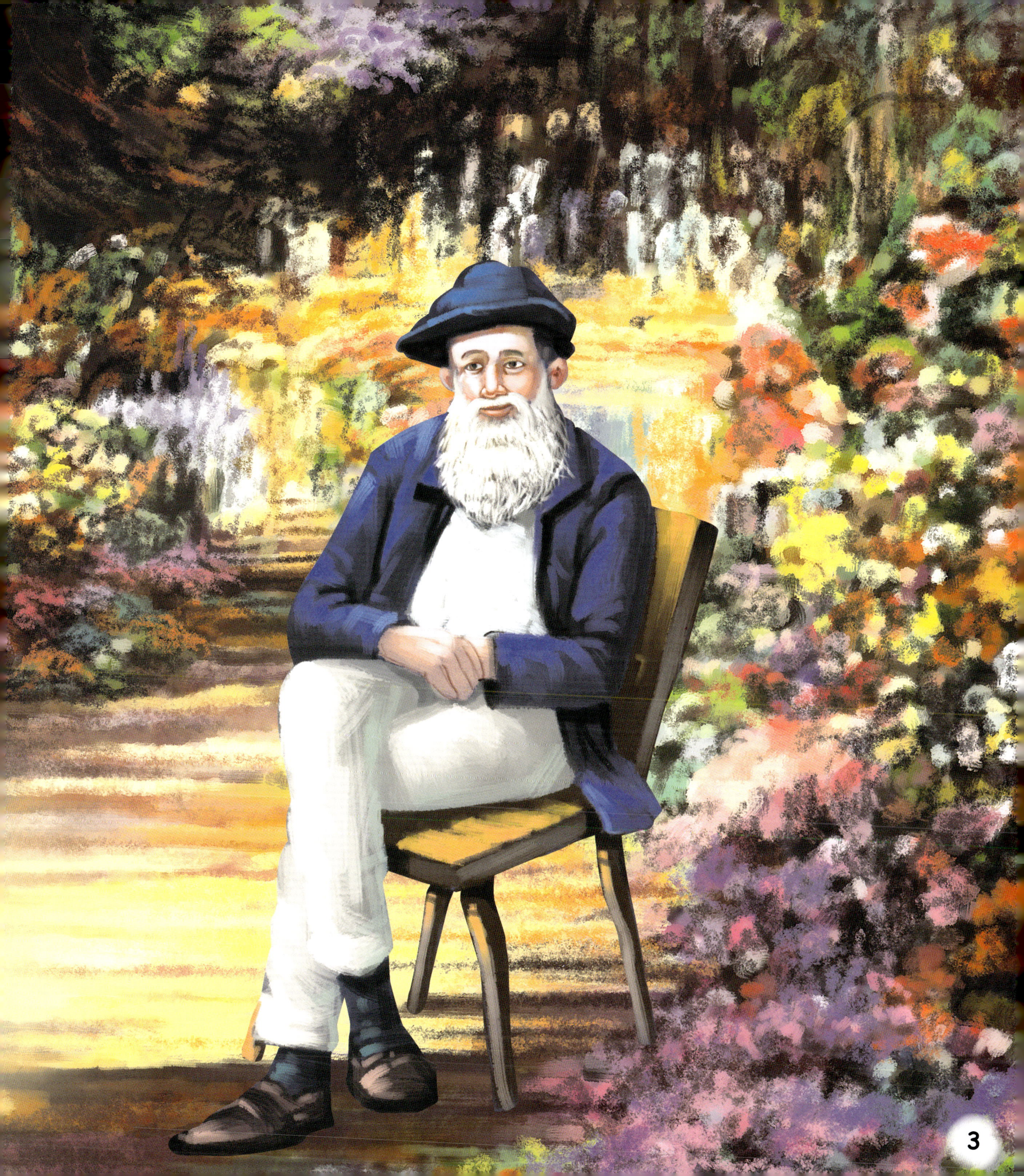

As a child, Monet did not like school very much, but he loved to draw. He spent most of his time drawing caricatures. People who had a good sense of humour paid him to draw funny pictures of themselves.

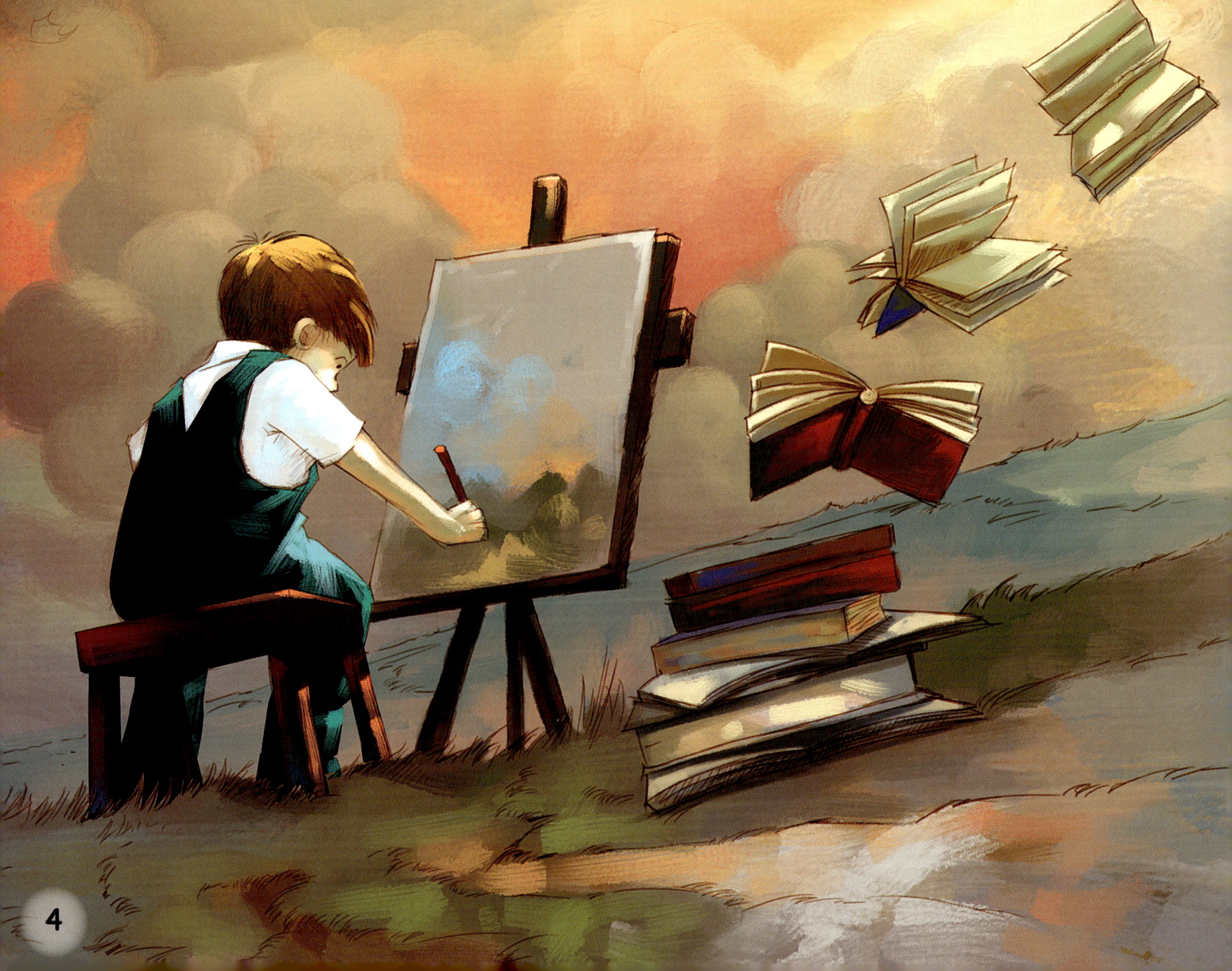

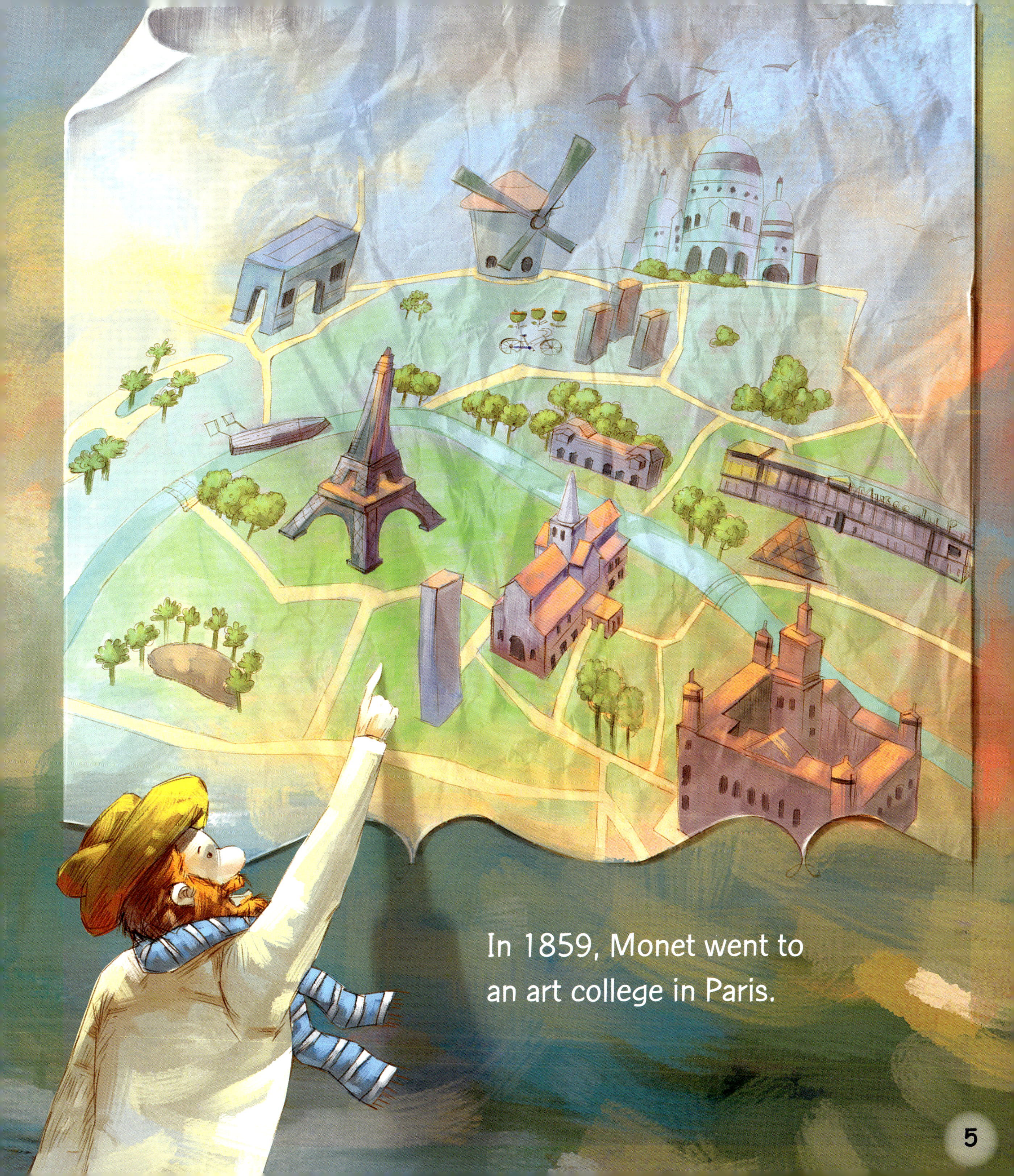

In 1859, Monet went to
an art college in Paris.

Once there, he made friends with other painters including Pierre-Auguste Renoir, Alfred Sisley and Frédéric Bazille.

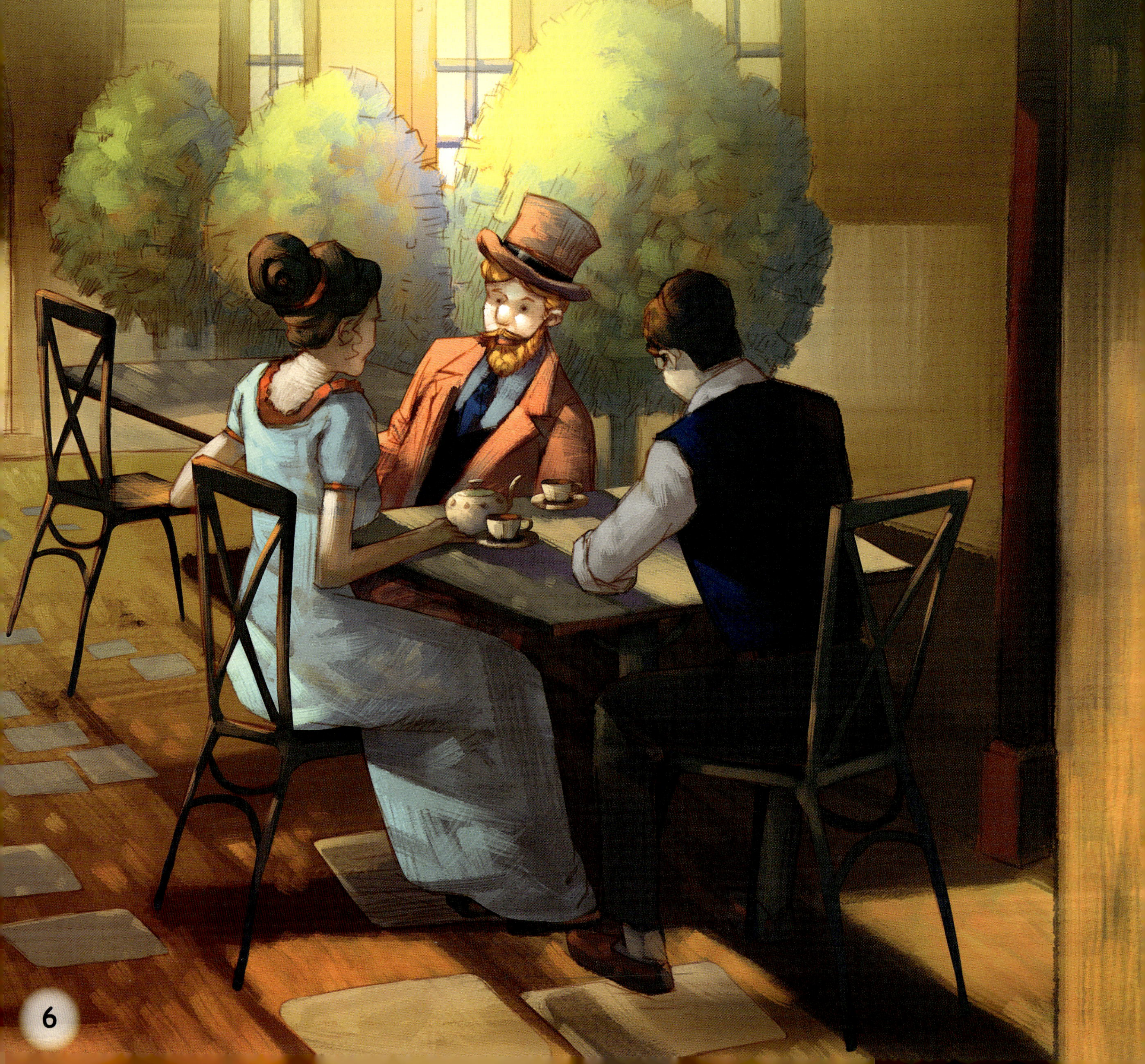

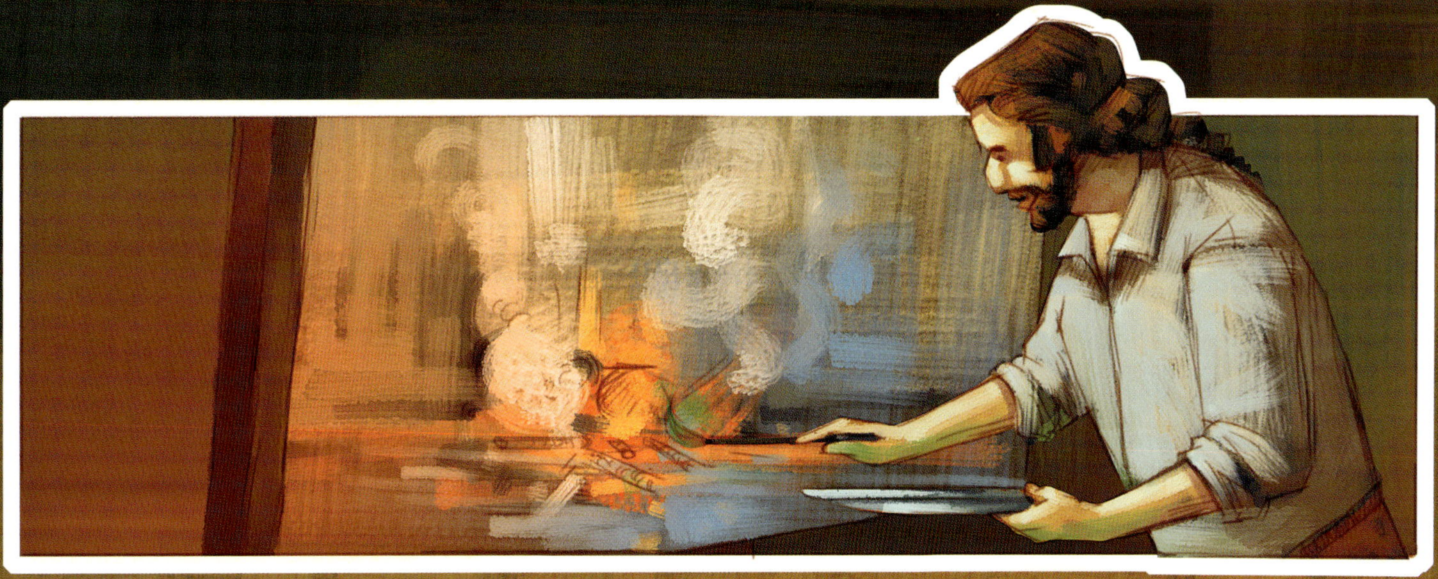

During this time, traditional painters worked in studios and created paintings that had clear outlines.

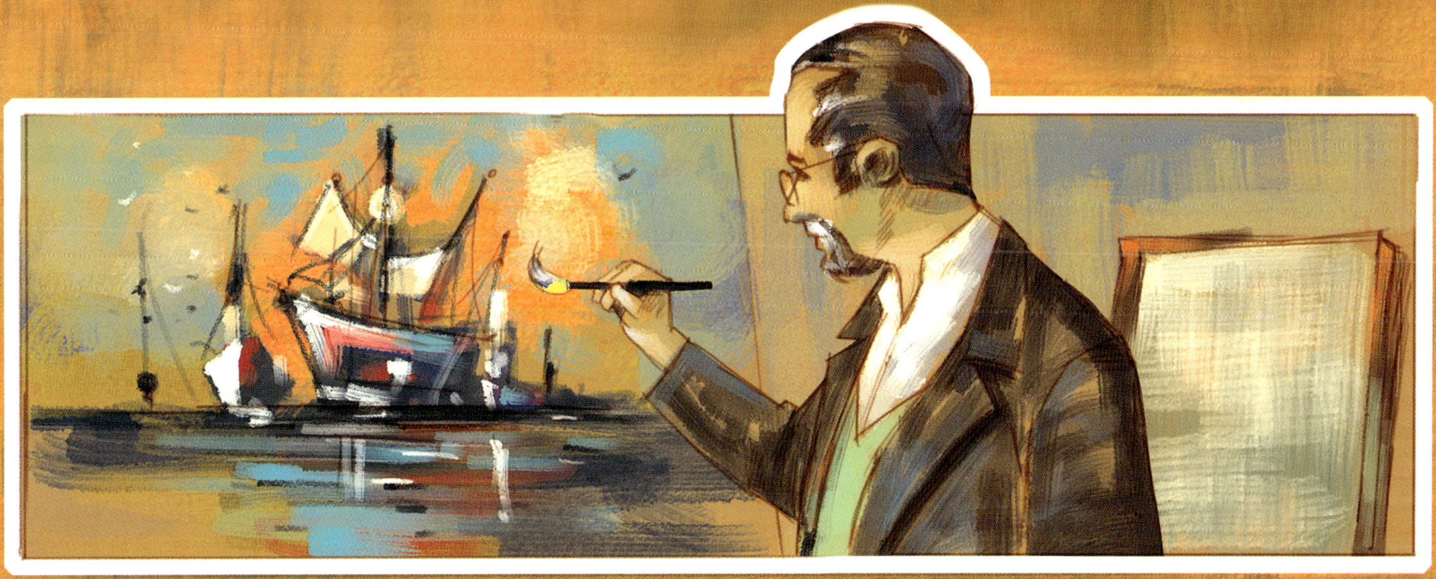

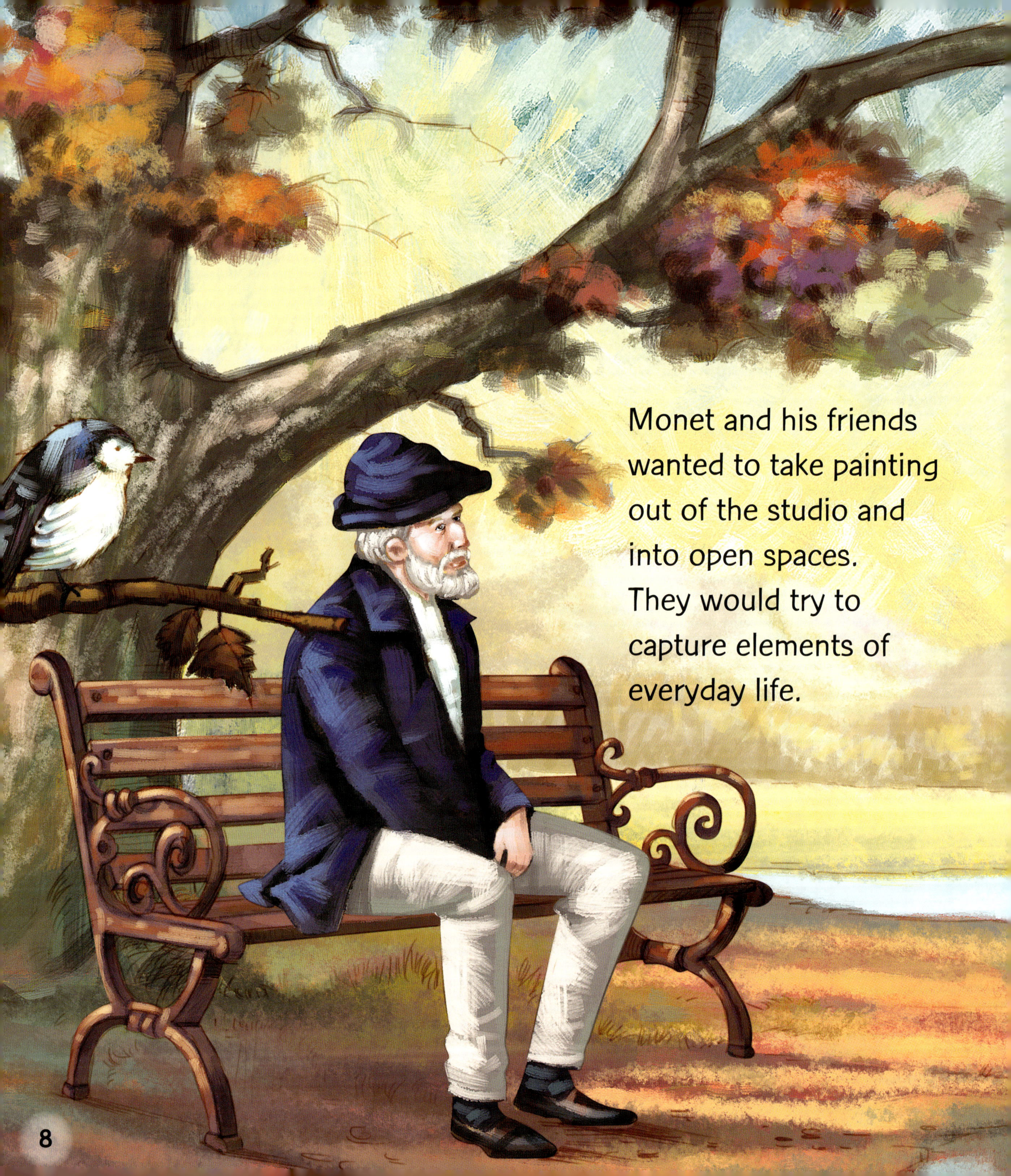

Monet and his friends wanted to take painting out of the studio and into open spaces. They would try to capture elements of everyday life.

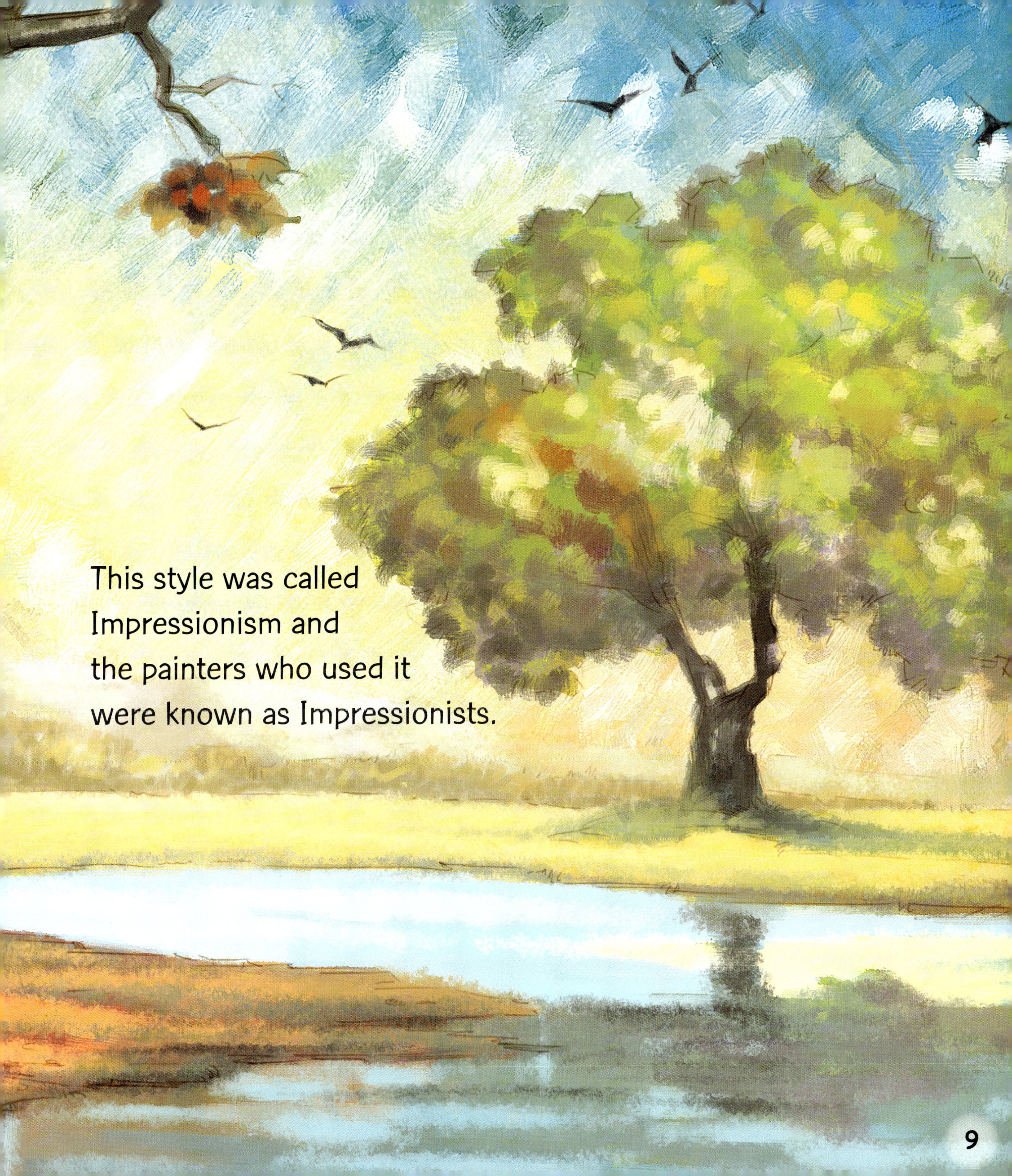

This style was called
Impressionism and
the painters who used it
were known as Impressionists.

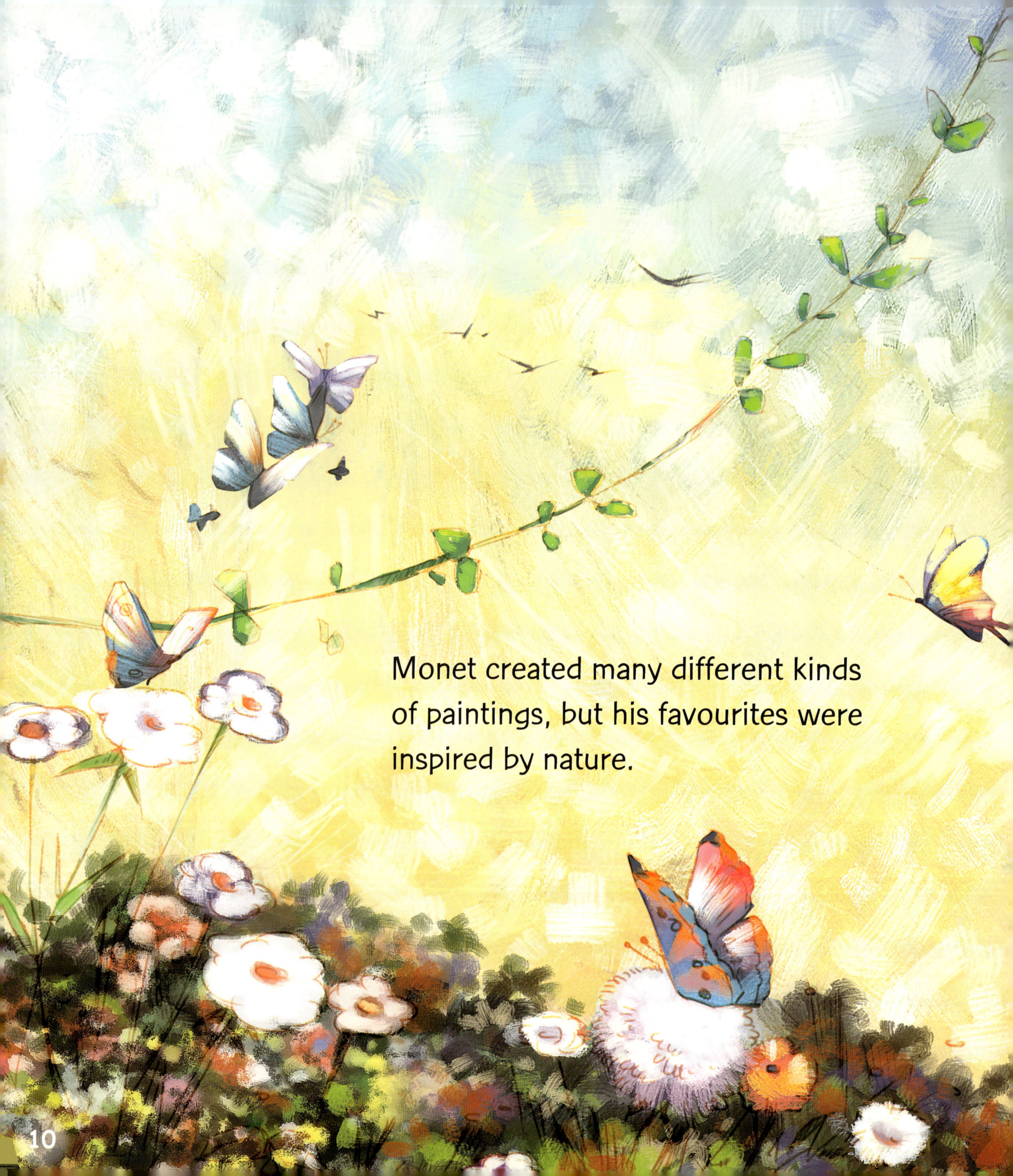

Monet created many different kinds of paintings, but his favourites were inspired by nature.

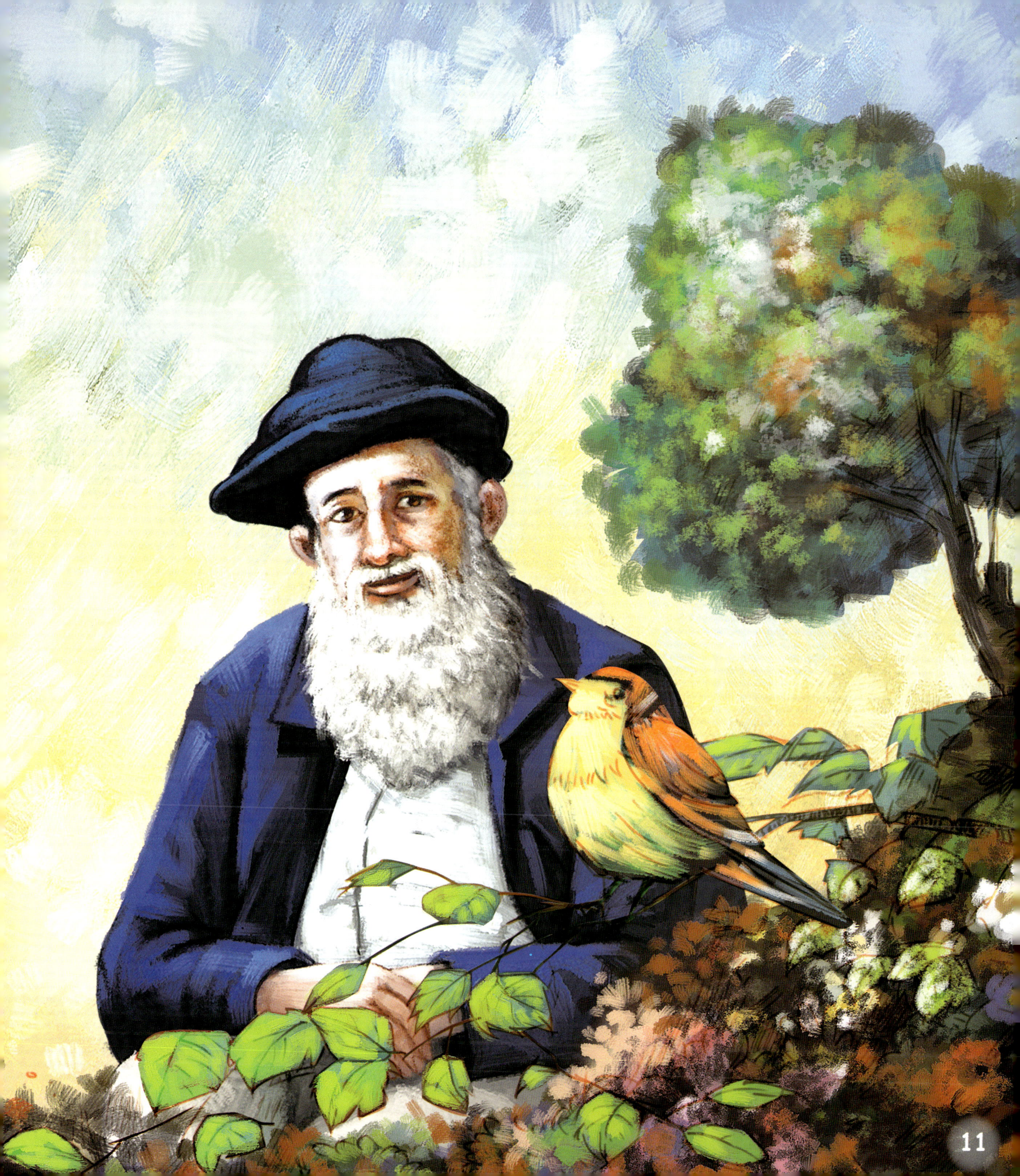

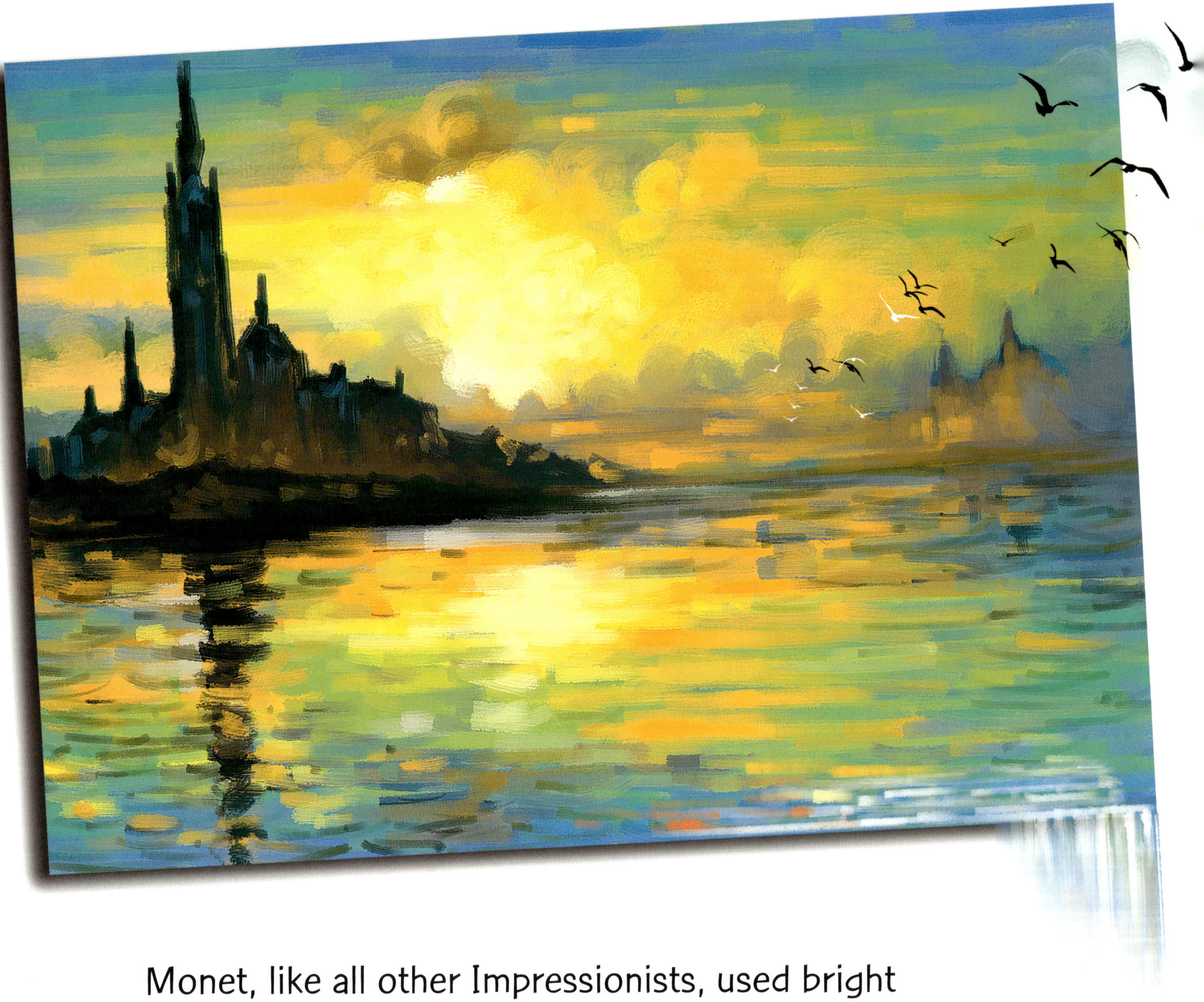

Monet, like all other Impressionists, used bright and simple colours and painted with thin and short but visible brushstrokes.

He would paint the same image at different times of the day to capture the changing effect of sunlight on objects.

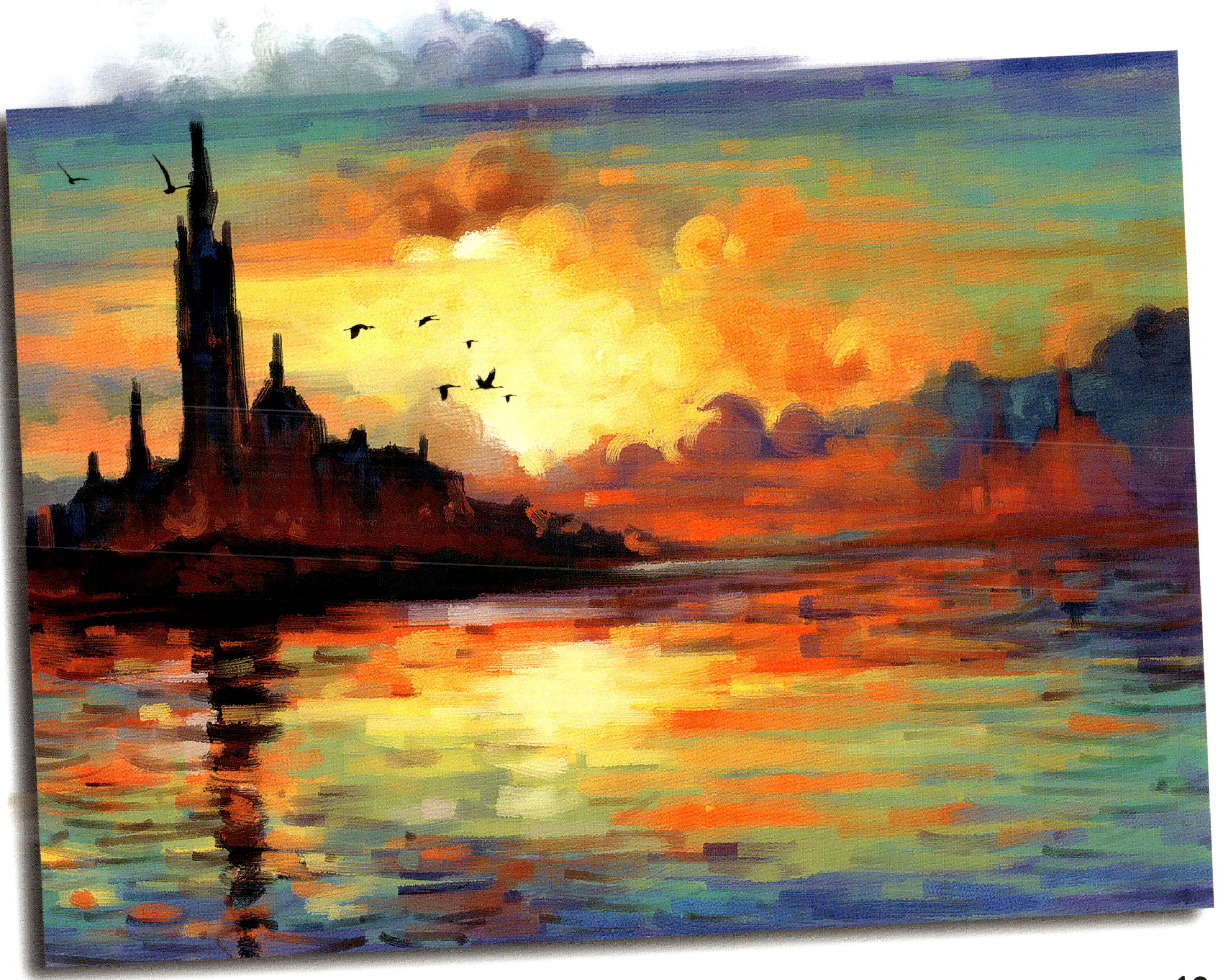

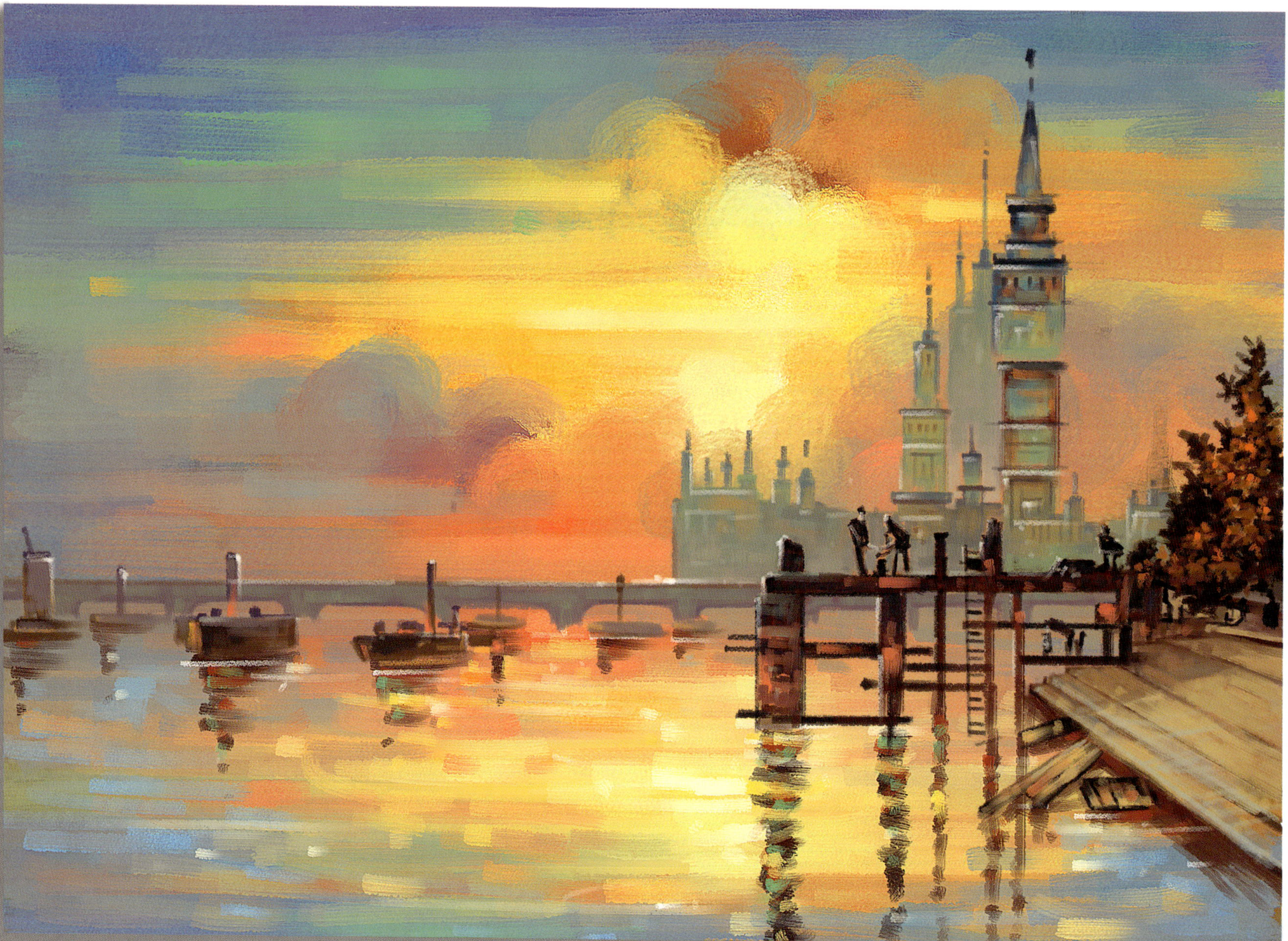

Monet's style of painting started to become popular at the American Impressionist Exhibition of 1886. He went on to become the most famous of all the Impressionist painters.

Some of Monet's most popular artworks were his series paintings, like the *Water Lilies* and the *Weeping Willows.*

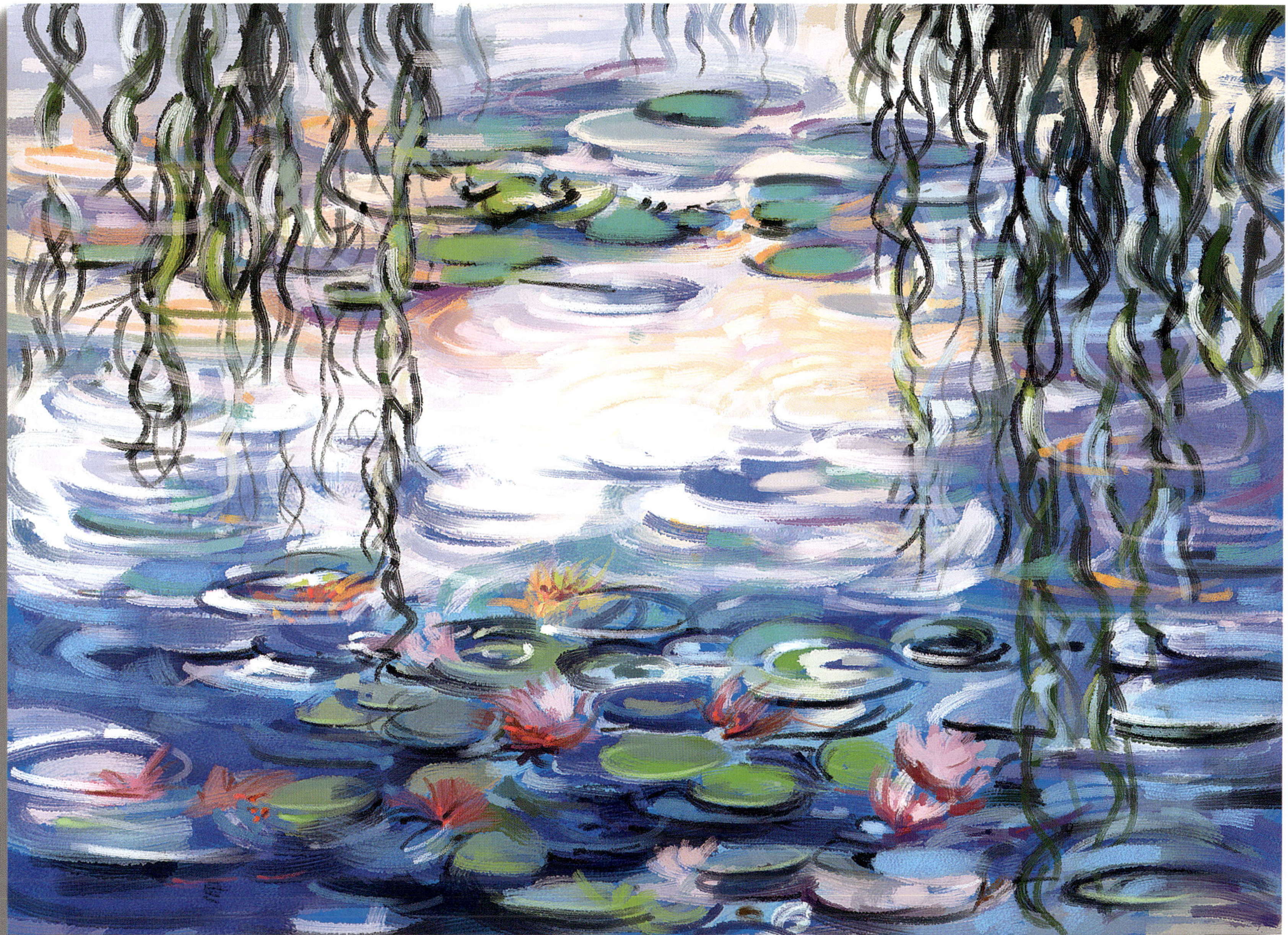

Monet died on 5 December, 1926, at the age of 86. He came to be known as the founder of French Impressionism, a movement that influenced many future artists.

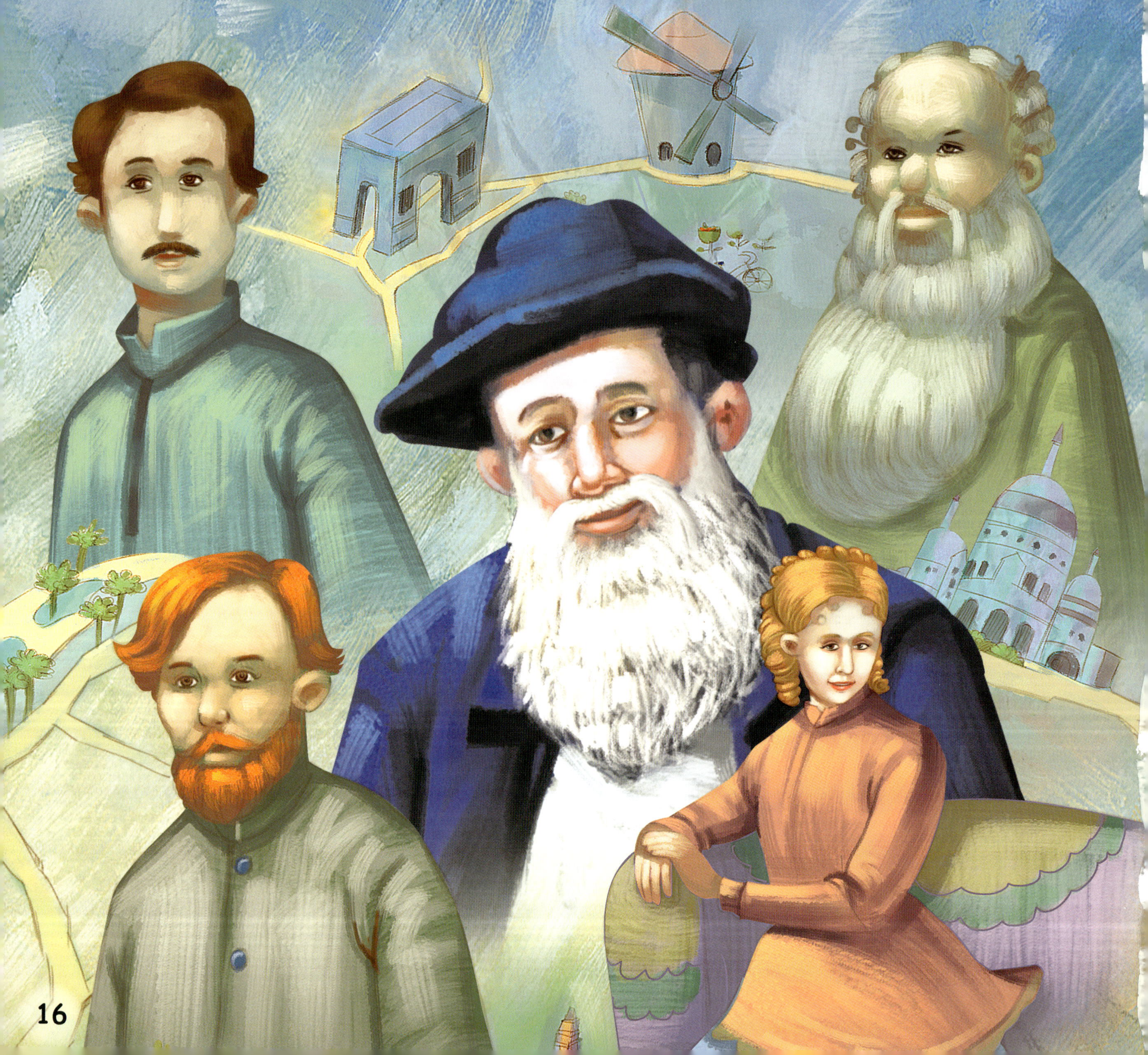